Polar Bears

by Molly Kolpin

Consultant:
Frank T. van Manen
Research Ecologist
U.S. Geological Survey
Leetown Science Center

CAPSTONE PRESS
a capstone imprint

First Facts is published by Capstone Press,
1710 Roe Crest Drive, North Mankato, Minnesota 56003.
www.capstonepub.com

 Books published by Capstone Press are manufactured with paper containing at least 10 percent post-consumer waste.

Library of Congress Cataloging-in-Publication Data
Kolpin, Molly.
 Polar bears / by Molly Kolpin.
   p. cm. — (First facts. Bears)
 Includes bibliographical references and index.
 Summary: "Discusses polar bears, including their physical features, habitat, range, and
life cycle"—Provided by publisher.
 ISBN 978-1-4296-6130-0 (library binding)
 ISBN 978-1-4296-7189-7 (paperback)
 1. Polar bear—Juvenile literature. I. Title. II. Series.
 QL737.C27K654 2012
 599.786—dc22

                                        2011001586

Editorial Credits
Christine Peterson, editor; Kyle Grenz, designer; Laura Manthe, production specialist

Photo Credits
Alamy: Danita Delimont/Thomas Mangelsen, 9, John Schwieder, 15, Juniors Bildarchiv,
13, Robert Harding Picture Library Ltd, 17; Corel, 1; Creatas, cover, 5, 19, 21; Minden
Pictures: Patricio Robles Gil, 10; PhotoAlto, 7; Photodisc, 20; Super Stock Inc.: Design
Pics, 18

Artistic Effects
Shutterstock: Andrejs Pidjass, Feliks Kogan

Essential content terms are **bold** and are defined at the bottom of the spread where they
first appear.

Printed in the United States of America in North Mankato, Minnesota.

012012   006536CGVMI

Table of Contents

Living Large

Adult polar bears are the world's largest land **predators**. They can stand more than 8 feet (2.4 meters) tall. Male polar bears can weigh 770 to 1,500 pounds (350 to 680 kilograms). Female polar bears weigh about 550 pounds (250 kg). Some polar bears can eat 90 pounds (41 kg) of food in just one meal.

predator—an animal that hunts another animal for food

At Home in the Cold

Polar bears live in some of the coldest places on Earth. To **survive**, these giant bears have a thick layer of fat. A heavy coat of fur adds extra warmth. Fur on the bottom of their paws blocks the cold. The furry pads keep bears from slipping on the ice.

survive—to continue to live

paws

On the Move

Polar bears wander across ice sheets near the Arctic Ocean. In North America, both Canada and Alaska are home to polar bears.

In summer the ice sheets where polar bears roam start to melt. Polar bears then move to live on land until winter.

Fact!
Polar bears are so strong, they can pull beluga whales from the water.

The Nose Knows

A polar bear uses its strong sense of smell to find seals and other **prey**. It finds a ringed seal's breathing hole and gets ready for action. When a seal comes up for air, the bear attacks. The polar bear bites the seal's head and lifts it onto the ice.

prey—an animal hunted by another animal for food

Polar Plunge

Polar bears also attack seals from the water. They spot seals on small chunks of ice. In the water, polar bears use their large front paws to paddle toward the animals. They pounce on the ice and snatch seals with their sharp teeth and claws.

13

Warm Dens

Most polar bears hunt through the winter. But female polar bears that are going to have babies do not. Females dig cozy **dens** in the snow. They live and sleep inside the dens during winter.

den—a place where a wild animal lives

Polar Bear Cubs

Polar bear **cubs** are born in December or January. Usually two cubs are born at a time. At birth they weigh just over 1 pound (.5 kg). Newborn cubs are 13 inches (33 centimeters) in length. The tiny cubs drink their mother's milk. They snuggle against their mother for warmth.

cub—a young bear

Life Cycle of a Polar Bear

Newborn—At birth, cubs' eyes are shut, and they have a thin layer of hair.

Young—After eight months, young bears weigh about 100 pounds (45 kg).

polar bear cubs

Adult—Fully grown polar bears can be 10 feet (3 m) long.

A Cub's Life

In March or April, a mother polar bear leads her cubs out of their den. She carries the cubs through areas of deep snow and water.

Polar bear cubs learn to hunt and
protect themselves. But they take time
out to play. They wrestle and pretend
to fight. Then they lie on their bellies to
cool off when it's warm.

On Their Own

Young polar bears stay with their mother for about two years. Then the young bears can hunt on their own. Polar bears can live for 30 years, but most live about 15 to 18 years.

Amazing but True!

Polar bears are known for their white fur. But their fur isn't really white. It's clear! Each hair is a colorless, hollow tube. The hairs look white because of how they reflect light.

Glossary

cub (KUHB)—the young of a bear

den (DEN)—a place where a wild animal lives

predator (PRED-uh-tur)—an animal that hunts other animals for food

prey (PRAY)—an animal hunted by another animal for food

survive (sur-VIVE)—to continue to live

Read More

Landau, Elaine. *Polar Bears: Hunters of the Snow and Ice*. Animals of the Snow and Ice. Berkeley Heights, N.J.: Enslow Publishers, 2010.

Meinking, Mary. *Polar Bear vs. Seal*. Predator vs. Prey. Chicago: Raintree, 2011.

Sisk, Maeve T. *Polar Bears*. Animals That Live in the Tundra. New York: Gareth Stevens Pub., 2011.

Internet Sites

FactHound offers a safe, fun way to find Internet sites related to this book. All of the sites on FactHound have been researched by our staff.

Here's all you do:

Visit *www.facthound.com*

Type in this code: 9781429661300

Check out projects, games and lots more at
www.capstonekids.com

23

Index